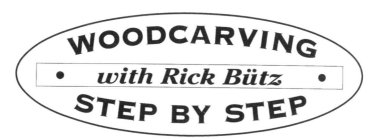

WOODCARVING
with Rick Bütz
STEP BY STEP

How to Sharpen Carving Tools

0   11557 02996   3

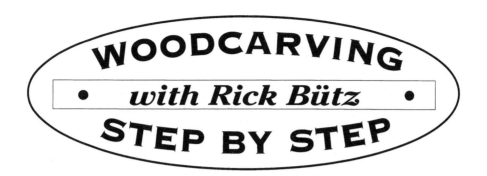

WOODCARVING
· with Rick Bütz ·
STEP BY STEP

How to Sharpen Carving Tools

Rick and Ellen Bütz

STACKPOLE
BOOKS

Copyright © 1997 by Rick and Ellen Bütz

Published by
STACKPOLE BOOKS
5067 Ritter Road
Mechanicsburg, PA 17055
www.stackpolebooks.com

Printed in the United States of America

10 9 8 7 6 5 4

FIRST EDITION

Cover design by Tracy Patterson with Wendy A. Reynolds

We have tried to make this book as accurate and correct as possible. Plans, illustrations, photographs, and text have been carefully researched. However, because of the variability of all local conditions, materials, personal skills, and so on, Stackpole Books and the authors assume no responsibility for any injuries suffered or damages or other losses incurred that result from material presented herein. Carefully study all instructions and plans before beginning any projects.

Library of Congress Cataloging-in-Publication Data

Bütz, Richard.
     How to sharpen carving tools / Rick and Ellen Bütz. — 1st ed.
         p. cm. — (Woodcarving step by step with Rick Bütz)
     ISBN 0-8117-2996-6
     1. Woodworking tools. 2. Sharpening of tools. I. Bütz, Ellen, 1950– . II. Title. III. Series: Bütz, Richard. Woodcarving step by step with Rick Bütz.
TT186.B88   1997
684'.08–DC20   96–38436
                                                                                                                CIP

ISBN 978-0-8117-2996-3

*To Tom and Carol
and all their sheep*

Contents

Sharpening Materials
1

Knives
5

Gouges
21

Chisels, V-Gouges, and Veiners
45

Care of Tools
73

Resources
83

Sharpening woodcarving tools isn't hard to learn. It just takes the right technique and a little practice.

Sharpening Materials

SHARPENING IS THE REAL SECRET OF WOODCARVING. Sharp tools make carving safer, more efficient, and most important, more fun.

A sharp tool glides through the wood leaving a smooth, polished surface behind. A carving made with sharp tools has a crisp, professional look. Dull tools leave a crushed and splintered surface that makes even the most beautifully designed and carefully worked carving look crude and unfinished.

Sharp tools are also safer. It takes less force to move the tool through the wood, and it's easier to control too. A perfectly sharp blade is less likely to slip and cause trouble.

But most of all, sharp tools make carving more enjoyable. They free you to concentrate on the creative process of carving without the frustration of trying to force your way with dull tools.

In theory, sharpening is simple: you just wear away enough metal on the cutting edge of a tool to leave it razor sharp.

In practice, however, it quickly becomes complicated. There is an enormous variety of sharpening materials available today, including dozens of different stones, lubricants, and mechanical sharpening devices. And it won't take you long to discover that individual carvers have their own methods of sharpening. To add to the confusion they will all tell you that their way is the only correct way.

In truth, there is no one right way to sharpen. Any method that is safe and leaves your tool razor sharp and ready to carve is perfectly acceptable.

I've experimented with many different techniques and materials for more than thirty years and have developed a sharpening method that is safe, simple, and effective. It combines centuries-

India sharpening stone with red cedar storage box

SHARPENING MATERIALS

Procedure	Material	Description	Use
Whetting	India oilstone	Hard, reddish orange fine stone made from aluminum oxide (400 grit)	Used to shape the bevel and produce a burr edge
Honing	Hard white or black Arkansas slip stone or	Hard, very fine natural stone from the mineral noviculite (800 to 1000 grit)	Used to remove the burr edge on gouges
	White ceramic slip stones	Very hard, fine, man-made abrasive stone (1000 grit)	
Polishing	Strop and dry abrasive	Leather surface coated with very fine abrasive powder (about 2000 grit)	Used to remove the burr edge and polish the blade to a razor-sharp cutting edge

old honing techniques with the best modern materials.

This method is inexpensive and requires only a few materials: a sharpening stone, honing oil, a few slip stones, a leather strop, and some patience. The different sharpening gadgets, like power honing wheels and angle jigs, are interesting, but are not necessary for producing perfectly sharp tools. In addition, many of these devices are intended for cabinetmaking tools such as planes and bench chisels, which require a different kind of cutting edge than is suitable for woodcarving. I recommend mastering my sharpening method before you buy a lot of expensive equipment.

Your sharpening stone should have a medium-fine grit and be about 2 inches wide and 8 inches long. I strongly recommend a man-made stone of fused aluminum oxide called an India stone, made by the Norton Company. It acquired the name India stone decades ago because it resembles a natural stone originally found in India. This type of sharpening stone has two sides: a coarse black side and a finer orange side. The fine side is used for the initial sharpening, or whetting, of the tool. The coarse side is rarely used, except for reshaping a badly damaged edge. India stones can be found in most hardware stores or woodworking supply catalogs. They are relatively inexpensive and will last many years if properly cared for.

Sharpening stones also need a lubricant to improve the cutting action of the abrasive against metal. Some types of stones use water, although India stones work best with oil. I prefer 3-in-One household oil. It is easy to obtain and has just the right amount of body. Specialized honing oils are available, but they don't really seem to make any noticeable difference.

The oil is important, because it lubricates the blade on the stone and floats away the tiny particles of metal as they are ground off. Without the oil, these metal filings would coat the surface of the stone and clog the pores of the abrasive. Eventually this would reduce the sharpening ability of the stone in a process called glazing.

To protect my sharpening stones, I keep them in wooden boxes. Red cedar is a good material because it has its own natural oil and resists soaking up the oil from the sharpening stone. The box should have a lid to keep wood shavings and dust off the surface of the stone when you are not using it.

You will also need a few slip stones of very fine grits for honing the blade of a tool after the initial whetting on an India stone. Slip stones are small sharpening stones that come in a variety of different shapes. They can be made from man-made materials or from natural stone, such as the Arkansas stones. For many decades these honing stones, mined near Hot Springs, Arkansas, were considered to be among the finest sharpening stones you could buy. The best-quality stones are becoming scarce and expensive, however. If you use natural stones for honing, use only fine hard white or black Arkansas stones. They should have an even color and appear translucent, almost like fine porcelain, when held up to the light. Avoid stones that look opaque and chalky.

Recent alternatives to the natural Arkansas stones are fine, white slip stones made of modern ceramic materials. These man-made stones are very smooth, hard, and even in texture. They are available in a variety of shapes and make superb slip stones. They can be purchased in a set containing all the shapes you need and are relatively inexpensive.

Slip stones come in a variety of shapes and materials. *From left to right:* **a fine India stone, a hard black Arkansas stone, two hard white Arkansas stones, two ceramic stones.**

Two types of leather strops and a block of fine abrasive

A strop is a piece of leather with a very fine abrasive grit rubbed into it. Strops are used for the final polishing of the blade after you have worked it on the stones. Strops are available from woodworking supply stores and catalogs. You can also make your own by tacking a strip of belt leather, suede side up, to a piece of scrap wood. I use a strop that I designed with one rounded edge and one angled edge. This makes it handy for stropping many different kinds of carving tools.

Although you can use the leather plain, adding some fine abrasive will make the polishing step go much faster. There are many compounds, such as jeweler's rouge, available for dressing a strop. I prefer an abrasive that is fine and dry. A waxy abrasive will build up on the strop and have to be cleaned off periodically. Oil-based abrasives like valve-grinding compound tend to be messy and can dissolve the adhesive that fastens the leather to the wood on a commercial strop.

My favorite abrasive is Yellowstone, a peach-colored compound that looks like a large rectangular piece of gritty chalk. It is fine, dry, fastcutting and doesn't build up on the strop.

These are the only supplies you need to sharpen all your carving tools. In the following chapters I will show you how to use these few simple materials to produce perfect cutting edges on any type of carving tool. If you follow the techniques described in this book to the letter, you will have safe, sharp tools and enjoy carving more.

Knives

KNIVES ARE THE MOST BASIC AND USEFUL OF ALL carving tools. Just about every carver starts out whittling with a knife. I can still remember getting my first real pocketknife. It was big and clumsy, and the rough handle raised blisters on my hand, but I loved it. In fact, I still have it, even though I don't use it much for carving anymore.

Knives are the best tools to begin carving with. Working with a knife develops skill and coordination. Carving with a knife also develops a feeling for carving with the grain of the wood. As you work with a knife on a small project, you quickly develop an intuitive sense of which type of cut produces a smooth, clean shaving and which splits off a chunk of wood you wanted to keep.

A good knife is the most versatile carving tool around. Many beautiful and intricate carvings can be created using just a knife. I use carving knives for making small figures like Santa Clauses and for wildlife carvings such as songbirds and small animals. Knives are the only tools used for the traditional European style of incised carving called chip carving. Knives are also handy for making fine detailing cuts on large sculptures and relief carvings created with gouges.

There are many different styles of carving knives. I prefer a knife with a short blade about 1¼ to 1½ inches long. A short blade gives you the best control for roughing out, as well as for carving details. The blade should be good-quality carbon steel to take a keen edge and hold it. Avoid stainless steel, which has a high chromium content and tends to dull more quickly.

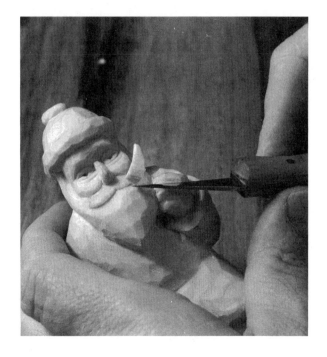

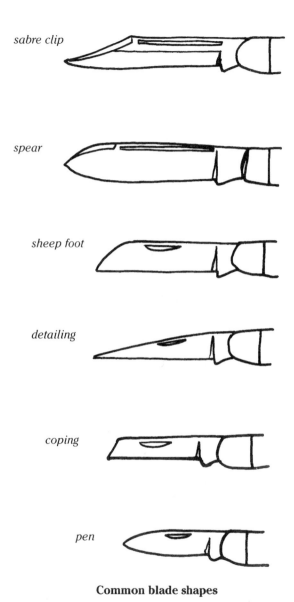

sabre clip

spear

sheep foot

detailing

coping

pen

Common blade shapes

My favorite blade shape is called a sheep foot pattern; it has a straight cutting edge that is easy to control. For carving fine details I also use a tapered, pointed detailing blade, which makes it easier to position the blade precisely in the wood.

Some carvers prefer different blade shapes. This is largely a matter of personal preference, so don't be afraid to experiment and find which shape works best for you. I recommend starting with one carving knife and getting the feel of it before adding other knives to your collection. Most carvers use just one or two favorite knives 90 percent of the time.

Many beautiful carvings have been made with

Wooden-handled carving and detailing knives, folding pocket knife.

folding pocketknives; however, I find a knife with a smooth, wooden handle more comfortable, especially if I am carving for long periods of time. The finish on the wooden handle is important too. An oil finish is less likely to raise blisters than a heavy lacquer or varnish finish. These tend to trap moisture from your skin and increase friction. The handle should fit your hand and feel comfortable in your grip.

Because of the simple shape of the blade, knives are the best woodcarving tools on which to learn sharpening. Once you have mastered knife sharpening, the same basic principles apply to sharpening every other type of carving tool.

Begin sharpening by placing a few drops of light oil on the fine (orange) side of an India combination stone.

Hold the sharp edge of the knife blade on the stone at a 20- to 25-degree angle. Don't worry about trying to measure this angle precisely. Just lay the knife blade flat on the stone and then raise the back edge enough to slide the point of a sharp pencil or the edge of a dime under it. The exact angle is not as important as keeping the angle constant as you work the knife on the stone. Changing the angle as you work may round the edge of the knife and lessen its carving efficiency.

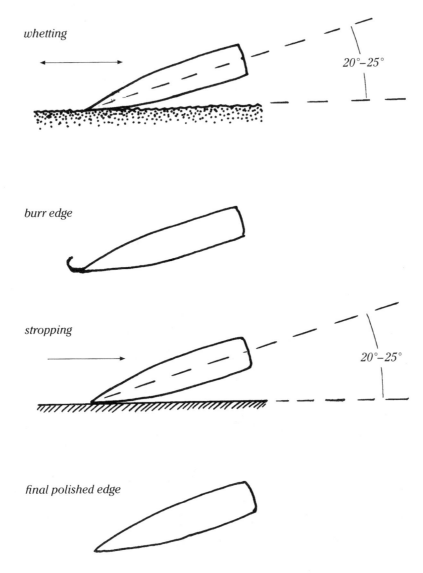

whetting

20°–25°

burr edge

stropping

20°–25°

final polished edge

Sharpening steps for a knife

Now slide the knife back and forth with steady, medium-firm pressure. Press about as hard as you do when writing with a ball-point pen.

After a few minutes, turn the blade over, position the knife at the same angle, and sharpen the other side. Try to work the knife equally on both sides.

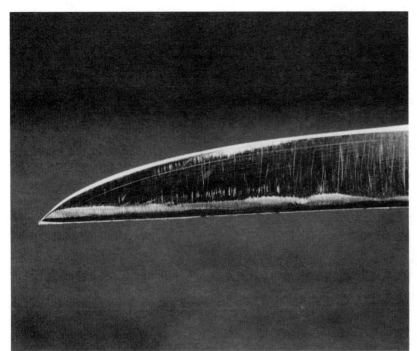

As you sharpen, you will notice a thin foil of metal called a burr edge beginning to develop along the cutting edge of the blade.

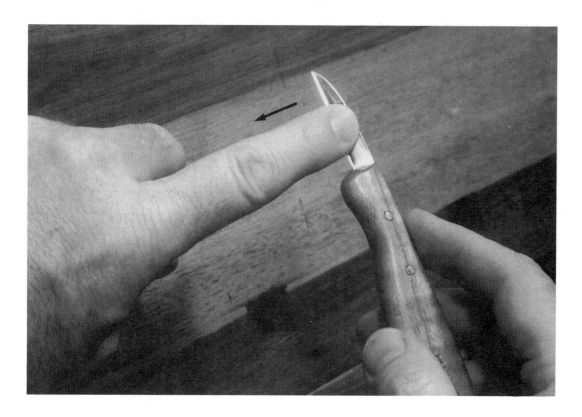

Sometimes you can see the burr edge as a thin line of light along the cutting edge. More often it is so small as to be nearly invisible. You can test for it by very lightly stroking your finger across the blade *away* from the cutting edge. The burr will catch in the ridges of your fingerprints and you will feel a slight, rough, tugging sensation.

Work the knife on the stone until you can feel a burr edge along the entire length of the blade. This may take anywhere from ten to twenty minutes. Once this burr edge has developed, the knife is as sharp as you can make it on the sharpening stone. You have completed the first step, and you can put your sharpening stone away.

The blade still needs work before you can carve with it, however. If you try carving with the burr edge still attached, it will break off or bend over, leaving you with a dull, ragged cutting edge. The burr edge has to be worn away smoothly to create a perfect cutting edge.

Stropping

The best way to remove the burr on a knife is to use a strop, a strip of leather with some abrasive grit rubbed into it. Hold the knife on the strop at the same angle you held it on the sharpening stone, 20 to 25 degrees. Stroke the knife along the leather in a smooth, steady movement in a direction *away* from the cutting edge. If you go the wrong way, the knife will cut into the leather, damaging it as well as dulling the knife.

Be sure to maintain the same angle and pressure for the entire length of the stroke. Be especially careful as you reach the end of a stroke to lift the knife off the strop cleanly. Avoid the temptation to imitate the old-time barbers who stropped their razors in a rapid back and forth motion. They were using a hollow ground straight razor, which required a different technique. If you try this with your carving knife, you may inadvertently change the angle, dragging the cutting edge across the strop at the end of each stroke. This will dull the blade, and you will need to resharpen it on the stone.

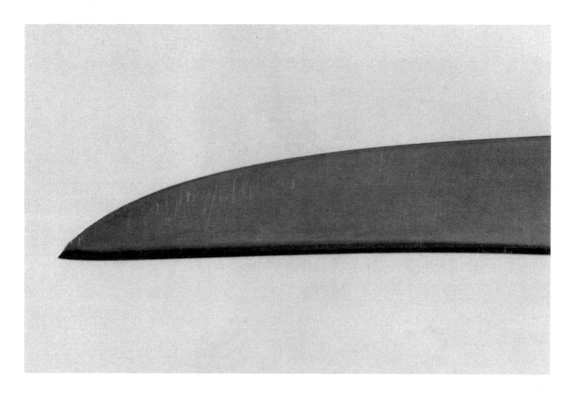

I like to strop for about a dozen strokes on one side, then lift the blade clear and strop the other side for a dozen strokes. Continue stropping both sides evenly until every trace of the burr edge is gone. This can take fifteen to thirty minutes or longer. It's time well spent, and as you gain experience it goes more quickly. The first time I got a truly sharp edge on my knife, it took me well over an hour. The next time it took only half that, and now, with luck, I can get a perfect edge in ten to fifteen minutes.

Stropping is also useful for resharpening the knife when it begins to dull from use. Usually a carbon steel blade will stay sharp for a couple of weeks with constant use, longer if you only carve occasionally. When you notice your knife beginning to dull slightly, just repeat the stropping procedure to restore a razor-sharp edge. You can touch up the edge several times on the strop before you need to whet it on the stone again.

Testing for Sharpness

At this point, you should have a perfectly sharpened razor edge on your knife. But before you begin carving, test it to make sure.

There are two ways to test a knife for sharpness. The first is to rest the blade lightly on your fingernail. Don't exert any pressure at all—you are not trying to carve your fingernail! Just use a light delicate touch. If the blade slides across the surface of your nail, the cutting edge needs more work. If it feels sticky on your fingernail and doesn't slide around, the blade is razor sharp and ready to carve. This is a very sensitive test. With practice you will be able to tell instantly if any part of the blade is sharp or needs more work.

Never rub your thumb or finger across or along the blade to test for sharpness as you may see others do. Besides being dangerous, this is not an accurate test for sharpness. A blade that is too dull for carving can still cut you.

Another test for sharpness is to make a practice cut across the end grain on a small block of softwood such as white pine or basswood. The end grain is the part of the wood where the annual growth rings show, and a knife has to be razor sharp to cut it cleanly and smoothly.

If the knife makes a crunching sound and tears the wood off in ragged splinters, it is not sharp enough. Usually this just means you need to continue stropping the blade some more.

A sharp knife will slice through the wood with a soft whistling sound, removing clean shavings and leaving a smooth, polished surface behind. Test the blade along its entire length to make sure it is sharp right to the tip.

Troubleshooting

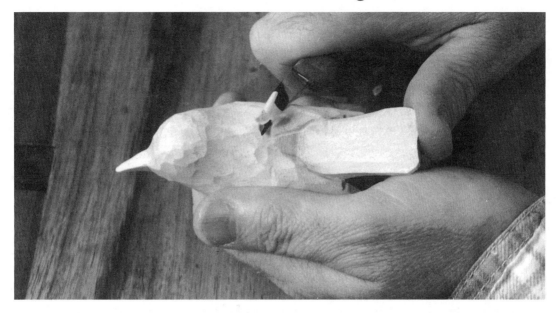

This sharpening method has one major advantage over all others: it is easy to diagnose and correct your mistakes. For instance, if you can't raise a burr edge as you whet the knife on the India stone, you probably are not applying enough pressure. Try again, using a medium-firm pressure. Be sure to maintain a constant angle as you work the knife on the stone.

If your knife forms a large burr at the tip and little or none near the handle, you are putting too much pressure on the tip as you sharpen. Work at keeping the pressure equal along the entire length of the blade.

When you can feel a burr along the full length of the blade, you know that you have sharpened it properly on the stone. Then, if the knife doesn't pass the sharpness test when you have finished stropping, you know the problem is in your stropping technique.

There are two common stropping problems. The first is simply not doing it long enough. If your knife tests as dull, check for remnants of a burr edge and continue stropping until they are all removed.

The second problem is not maintaining a consistent angle as you strop. Be especially careful not to let the angle change and drag the cutting edge of the blade across the strop as you finish a stroke. This will dull the blade, and you may have to go back to the sharpening stone and raise a new burr edge.

Carving Safely with a Knife

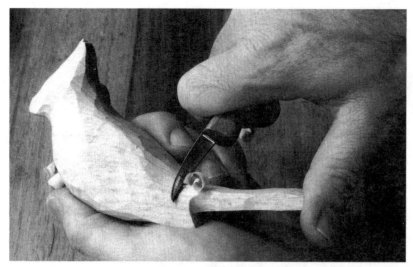

Before you begin carving with your newly sharpened knife, here are a few tips for using it safely.

There are two safe ways to carve with a knife. The first is called the paring cut because the basic motion is like peeling a potato. Brace your thumb on the carving and slowly close your hand as you draw the knife through the wood. Position your thumb on the carving so that the knife will not touch it as it cuts through the wood.

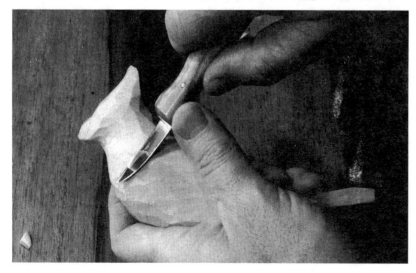

The second, called the levering cut, is handy for reaching places that are hard to carve with the paring cut. Brace the thumb of your left hand against the back of the knife blade and pivot the knife using your left thumb as a fulcrum.

These two methods are the best for removing wood safely. They also give you excellent control over the knife so that you can shape your carving exactly the way you want to. If you are left-handed, just reverse the hand positions. If you are just learning, these techniques may feel awkward at first; but take your time, and eventually they will become second nature.

For safety, relax and go slowly. Don't try to remove big chunks of wood with a single cut. Remember the old woodcarver's saying: "Three small chips are better than one big one."

Above all, *never* hold the wood in one hand and pull the knife toward you with the full force of your arm. This is very dangerous, because you have no control over the knife. Remember, wood-carving is a process of removing small chips of wood with control and precision. When carving, always keep the fingers of both hands braced on the wood for the greatest control and safety. The paring cut and levering cut will allow you to do this.

Once you have mastered knife sharpening, you are ready to move on to other carving tools. The method is essentially the same for all of them; you simply modify the basic knife-sharpening technique to suit any shape or size of carving tool.

Gouges

WOODCARVING GOUGES HAVE A SPECIAL MYSTIQUE. For hundreds of years they have been the means by which artists transformed simple logs into works of art. From the dragon prows of the Viking ships to the bold and powerful icons of Gothic woodcarvers, gouges have remained virtually unchanged in shape and design. Lined up on a bench, well honed and ready to carve, they seem to recall an unhurried age when there was all the time in the world for fine hand craftsmanship.

Frequently carvers take a special interest in their collection of gouges, often personalizing the blades and handles to make the tools uniquely their own. This is just another example of the bond between artisans and their tools, an increasingly rare phenomenon in modern times.

For centuries, woodcarving gouges have been used to shape wood.

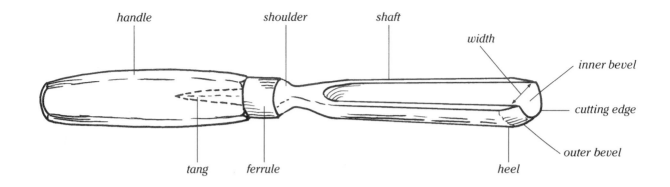

handle   shoulder   shaft   width   inner bevel   cutting edge   outer bevel   tang   ferrule   heel

Parts of a gouge

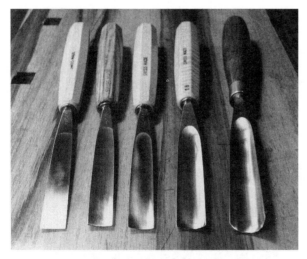

Cutting edges of gouges have different amounts of curvature called the sweep number. *From left to right:* no. 2, no. 3, no. 5, no. 7, no. 9.

Gouges have long blades sharpened at the tip and mounted in a wooden handle. Their shape makes it possible for them to scoop out wood in a way that knives cannot. They can remove large quantities of wood quickly and efficiently and are extremely versatile. They are used for relief carving, sculpture, and detailing smaller carvings.

Woodcarving gouges come in hundreds of different shapes and sizes. You really only need about a half dozen basic shapes to start with. As you gain experience, you can add more to your collection.

Gouges are measured in two ways. The first is the width across the cutting edge, usually measured in millimeters. The second is called the sweep, and it measures the amount of curvature of

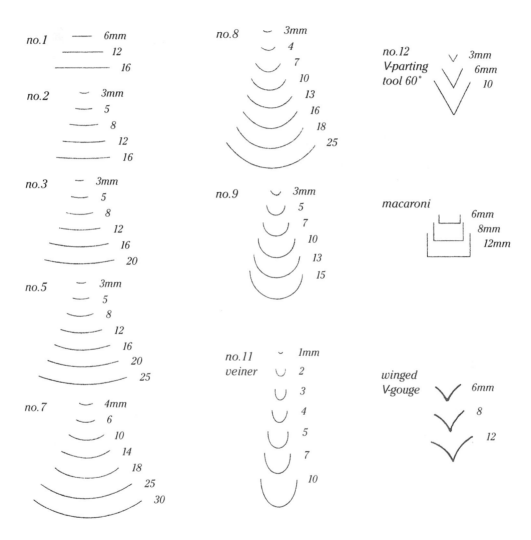

no.1 — 6mm
— 12
— 16

no.2 — 3mm
— 5
— 8
— 12
— 16

no.3 — 3mm
— 5
— 8
— 12
— 16
— 20

no.5 — 3mm
— 5
— 8
— 12
— 16
— 20
— 25

no.7 — 4mm
— 6
— 10
— 14
— 18
— 25
— 30

no.8 — 3mm
— 4
— 7
— 10
— 13
— 16
— 18
— 25

no.9 — 3mm
— 5
— 7
— 10
— 13
— 15

no.11 veiner — 1mm
— 2
— 3
— 4
— 5
— 7
— 10

no.12 V-parting tool 60° — 3mm
— 6mm
— 10

macaroni — 6mm
— 8mm
— 12mm

winged V-gouge — 6mm
— 8
— 12

Common gouge sizes and sweeps

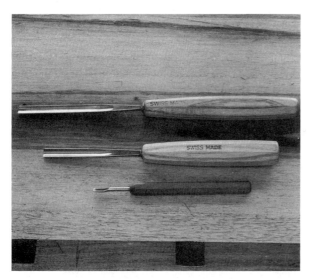

Gouges also come in different lengths. *From top to bottom:* **full size, student or intermediate size, micro gouge.**

A fishtail gouge has a more sharply tapered blade than a regular gouge.

the cutting edge. Sweep numbers vary somewhat among different manufacturers. Generally they range from a no. 1 gouge, which has a straight cutting edge, to a no. 11, whose cutting edge is curved into a U shape.

Gouges also vary in their overall length. A full or professional size is usually about 10 inches long, including both blade and handle. The smaller, lighter student or intermediate size is about 8 inches long. Tiny micro gouges, 5 inches long, are useful for carving fine details. I find each size useful in different situations and have some of each

in my tool collection. However, for starting out, the full-size, professional tools are the most versatile and provide the best control.

The shape of the blade can also vary. Some gouges have a wide cutting edge with a blade that tapers down to a narrow shaft, forming a triangular shape called a fishtail. Fishtail gouges are very handy for reaching into tight spaces where a full-width blade would not fit. There are also gouges on which the normally straight shaft is curved in varying degrees. But these are not commonly used tools, and they will be discussed later.

Whetting Gouges

The basic steps for sharpening a gouge are the same as for sharpening a knife. First use a sharpening stone to whet the blade and raise a burr edge, then remove the burr smoothly to leave a razor-sharp cutting edge. The details of the technique are slightly different, however, because of the curved shape of the cutting edge.

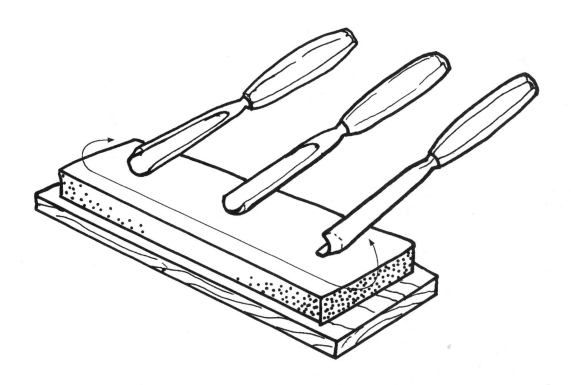

To sharpen a gouge, begin by putting a few drops of oil on an India combination stone. Then hold the blade on the stone at a 25- to 30-degree angle. Slide the blade along the length of the stone, rotating it as you go so that the entire cutting edge comes in contact with the stone. Work the blade on the stone with a rocking motion until a burr edge forms along the cutting edge just as it did on the knife.

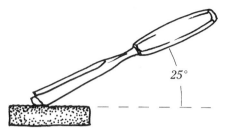

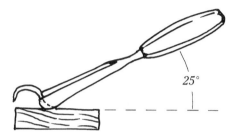

The sharpening angle is more critical with gouges than with knives. The angle at which you hold a gouge on the stone while sharpening will be the same angle at which the tool will cut wood when you are carving. In other words, if you hold the gouge at a 25-degree angle when you sharpen, the gouge will begin cutting the wood at 25 degrees when you carve. For straight gouges, an angle of 25 to 30 degrees will give you the most efficient carving action. This angle doesn't have to be exact, but try to get it as close as you can. With experience, your hands will be able to tell the correct angle just by feel.

Test the blade for a burr edge periodically by gently dragging your finger across the blade away from the cutting edge. This is the same test you used to check for a burr edge on the knife. When the burr extends along the entire length of the cutting edge, it is time for the next step, removing the burr edge.

Honing

Although you could remove the burr just by stropping the gouge on leather like a knife, it would take longer to strop the entire edge inside and out because of the curved cutting edge. Instead, I find it quicker and more efficient to use a slip stone to hone the edge of a gouge and remove most of the burr edge. Then I do the final polishing on a strop.

As mentioned earlier, slip stones are small, very fine sharpening stones that come in a variety of shapes and sizes. For removing the burr on a curved gouge, you need a rounded shape that will fit the inside curve of the blade. A small, rod-shaped, ceramic slip stone works perfectly.

A handy tip for breaking in either a hard Arkansas stone or a ceramic slip stone is to rub two of them together for a few moments to create an even finer honing surface. This also removes any minute surface irregularities.

Starting with the inner bevel, hold the slip stone against the blade at a 45-degree angle. Lightly pull the stone toward you, against the burr edge. Rotate the gouge slightly as you do this so that you can cover the entire edge.

Then repeat the procedure on the outer bevel.

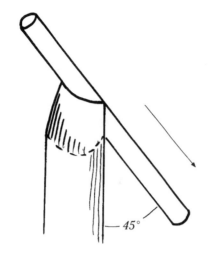

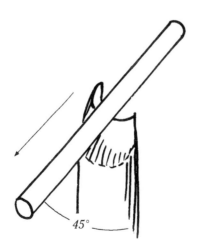

You need to work both the inner and outer surfaces of the gouge because remnants of the burr edge will often bend from the side you are working on to the other as you apply pressure. By stroking both sides of the gouge with the slip stone, you are sure to remove almost all of the burr. Usually three or four passes on each side will do the trick. Then you are ready to polish the edges with the strop.

Because of the slight pressure and fine grit of the slip, honing the gouge at a 45-degree angle doesn't affect the cutting angle of the tool. In a sense, what you are doing is creating a microbevel. This removes the burr quickly but does not alter the cutting angle. If you wish, you can also use this technique when sharpening a knife prior to stropping.

Stropping

Use a strop to polish the bevel to a perfect edge just as you did with the knife. Be sure to rub a little fine abrasive into the leather to speed the polishing action. Hold the gouge at a 25- to 30-degree angle to the strop, and draw it along the leather in a direction away from the cutting edge. Rotate the tool as you stroke it to bring the entire curved edge in contact with the strop.

Repeat this for several minutes, then turn the gouge over and polish the inside bevel on the rounded edge of the strop. If your strop doesn't have a rounded surface, you can use a folded piece of leather. Continue stropping both sides until you have a perfect razor-sharp cutting surface along the entire edge.

Stropping the bevel also polishes away the minute scratches left by the sharpening stone. This reduces friction as you carve. A well-polished gouge will seem to glide through the wood.

When the gouge begins to get slightly dull from use, you can touch up the edge by stropping it again for five or ten minutes. As with the knife, you can do this several times before you need to whet the tool again on the India stone.

Testing for Sharpness

You can check a gouge for sharpness by using the thumbnail test as you did with the knife. *Lightly* rest the cutting edge on your nail to see if it feels sticky. Test each part of the entire edge this way. Any places that are not sharp enough require extra stropping time.

Alternatively, use a piece of softwood like pine or basswood to test for sharpness. Make a practice cut across the grain of the board—in the direction perpendicular to the grain lines. A dull tool will crush and tear the fibers, making a crunching sound as you carve.

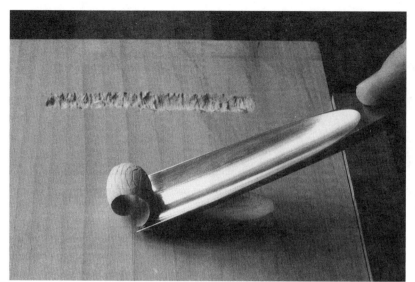

A sharp gouge, on the other hand, will sever the wood fibers cleanly, producing a nice curled shaving with a soft whistling sound.

A slightly dull tool may still carve a hardwood such as cherry or walnut just fine. A softwood, however, requires a perfect razor-sharp edge to carve smoothly, which makes it ideal to use for testing.

Troubleshooting

Most problems with sharpening gouges occur while whetting the tool on the India stone. If the tool is rolled too far, the corners can become rounded. Although this reduces the effective surface of the cutting edge, the gouge will still work; it just won't remove as much wood. Ideally, a gouge should have an even cutting edge perpendicular to the length of the shaft with square corners. Other irregularities can occur if part of the edge is whetted on the sharpening stone too long or with more pressure in one spot than another.

If you end up with an irregular edge, the best remedy is to start the sharpening procedure over from the beginning. To do this, first square up the edge by holding the gouge upright, or vertical, on the India sharpening stone. Rub the edge back and forth on the stone until it is even. Then begin sharpening again by whetting the gouge with a rocking motion as you did earlier.

One final note: gouges seem to carve better if the heel of the bevel, the place where the outside bevel meets the shaft of the tool, is rounded slightly. This helps the gouge make a smoother transition when it is coming out of the wood during a cut. Just whet a little metal off the heel by lowering the angle slightly and making a few passes with the India stone.

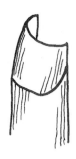

a correctly sharpened gouge has an even cutting edge perpendicular to the shaft and sharp corners

rounded corners are caused by rolling the gouge over too far when sharpening

an angled cutting edge results when the gouge is not rotated enough during whetting

an uneven cutting edge is caused by applying uneven pressure when rotating the gouge on the oil stone

Gouge sharpening problems

Sharpening Curved Gouges

Up to this point we have been discussing gouges with straight shafts. There is also a wide assortment of specialized gouges with shafts that are curved in varying amounts. These come in nearly all the sizes and sweeps of straight-bladed gouges. Curved gouges are used to remove wood in recesses that are difficult to reach with a straight gouge. They are not used all that often but can be very handy when you need them.

These gouges are sharpened the same way as regular straight gouges, except that you need to adjust the sharpening angle on the stone; this compensates for the curved shaft, which alters the cutting angle of the tool.

A front bent grounder has a slight S curve to the blade and is particularly favored by English woodcarvers. Although an uncommon shape, it is useful for smoothing the background, or lowest level, of a relief carving, especially when areas of the carving might obstruct a straight blade. Front bent grounders are usually sharpened at a 25- to 35-degree angle.

Shaft shapes *(from left to right):* straight, curved, front bent.

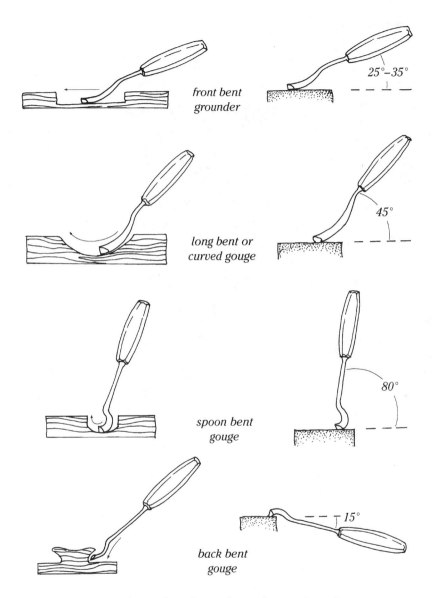

front bent
grounder

25°–35°

long bent or
curved gouge

45°

spoon bent
gouge

80°

back bent
gouge

15°

Sharpening angles and cutting actions of curved carving gouges

A long bent, or curved, gouge has a greater amount of curvature and is sharpened at a 45-degree angle. It is designed to hollow out concave surfaces such as the inside of a bowl or the underside of a bird's tail feathers.

The spoon bent gouge has a straight shaft with a deep curve just behind the cutting edge. This tool is useful for carving in deeply recessed areas that can't be reached with any other gouge. When carving in relief, hold the spoon gouge nearly vertical to prevent damage to adjacent areas of the woodcarving. Hold this gouge at approximately an 80-degree angle when sharpening.

Honing and polishing the inner bevel of a spoon gouge is slow and time-consuming because of the limited clearance between the cutting edge and the curved shaft. Use short strokes with a slip stone to remove most of the burr edge. Then use a piece of folded leather dressed with abrasive grit to polish the inner bevel. Luckily the spoon gouge is not used all that often, so you won't have to resharpen it frequently.

Another curved gouge is called a back bent. It is shaped like a spoon bent gouge except that the curve of the cutting edge is reversed. This shape makes it useful for undercutting raised portions of a carving. Traditionally it was used to cut away the wood underneath carved decorative leaves or similar relief designs. This makes the leaves appear more raised or separated from the background. Because of their unusual shape, back bent gouges are sharpened at an angle of 15 degrees *below* the surface of the oil stone. This is a very specialized shape, but it's useful when you need it.

One other oddly shaped tool you may encounter is a dog leg chisel. It has two right-angle bends in the shaft, and a single-beveled cutting edge like a cabinetmaker's chisel. A dog leg chisel is used to flatten the backgrounds on relief carvings by paring away excess wood. I rarely use this shape, although some carvers find it useful. Because the bevel is on the top side, the only trick to sharpening it is to hold it upside down at a 25-degree angle to the stone. Then, whet, hone, and polish the edge the same way as the others.

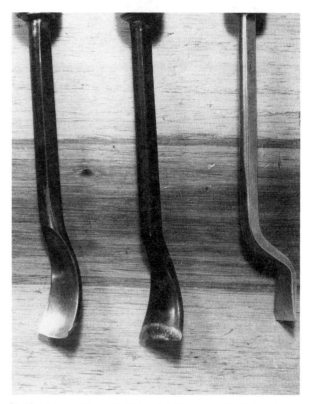

Shaft shapes *(from left to right):* **spoon, back bent, dog leg.**

Using Gouges Safely

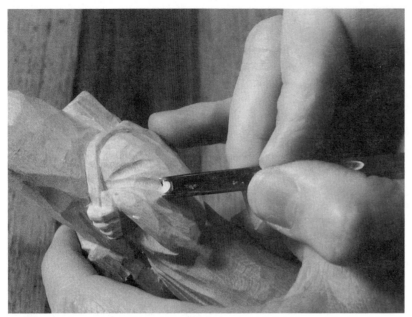

Woodcarving gouges are used in three different ways. For shaping fine details with a small gouge, usually less than 6mm in width, you can hold it in a pencil grip. Position the shaft of the tool like a pencil between your thumb and index finger. Use these two fingers to gently push the blade through the wood in a series of short cuts, while keeping your other fingers braced against the wood. For added safety, keep the fingers of the hand holding the carving out of the path of the tool. *Never* push the tool through the wood with the full force of your arm.

The next technique is the one you will use most of the time when making relief carvings or sculptures. First, fasten the piece of wood to a bench so that it will not move around. *Then hold the gouge with both hands,* positioning one hand on the handle to push the gouge and the other on the blade near the handle to guide the tool through the wood. For safety reasons, secure the carving to the bench. *Never hold a carving on a bench with one hand while you push a gouge through the wood with your other hand,* and always carve away from yourself. If you need to make a cut from the opposite direction, turn the carving around on the bench. *Never* pull the tool toward you.

Mallets come in a variety of sizes and materials.
Front: cocobolo. *Rear, from left to right:* **rubber, lignum vitae, hornbeam with an ash handle.**

It is a good idea to learn how to do this carving technique with either your right hand or left hand on the gouge handle. Practice switching your hand positions until you feel comfortable both ways. Learning to work ambidextrously will save you a lot of time in the long run. You will be able to reach more areas on your carving without having to reposition the wood on your bench.

If a gouge should happen to fall off your bench while you are working, do not try to catch it. Just get your feet out of the way and let it fall to the floor. By some perverse law of physics, dropped tools always seem to land point first. This phenomenon can provide you with many excellent opportunities to practice resharpening your gouges; this is better than risking injury by attemping to catch a tool in flight.

The third method for carving with gouges is to use a mallet to move the tool through the wood. This is usually done during the initial roughing out stage of a sculpture or relief carving. The extra power supplied by the mallet can remove a lot of waste wood quickly.

Mallets are traditionally made of dense woods like lignum vitae, a heavy tropical wood with interlocking fibers. Some modern versions combine a hardwood handle with a thick, synthetic rubber head. Mallets come in a variety of weights ranging from 10 to 30 or more ounces. I recommend a light to medium weight, about 20 ounces, to begin with.

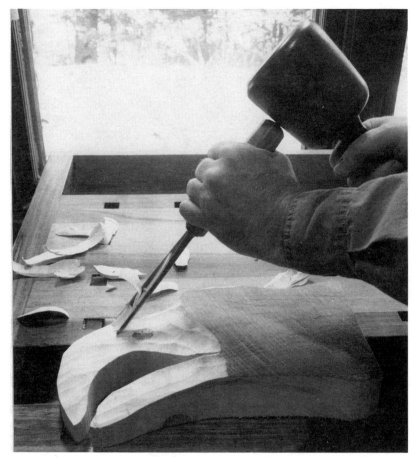

Use mallets to power the tool by lightly tapping the end of the handle. Don't swing the mallet with your whole arm the way you would a hammer. This is tiring and the motion is hard to control. Instead, hold the mallet close to the head and tap it against the tool with a small movement of your wrist and forearm. Use the other hand to guide the tool through the wood.

Never use a metal hammer on your woodcarving gouges. Metal doesn't have any resiliency or give. This will cause the tool handles to splinter and make them very uncomfortable to work with.

When using a gouge and mallet, make sure the carving is securely fastened to your bench, and *always* carve away from yourself. Take your time, and remove the wood in a series of small cuts rather than one big one. You'll work more safely and have better control of the carving process.

Chisels, V-Gouges, and Veiners

Besides all of the carving tools with curved sweeps, woodcarvers also use gouges that have straight cutting edges. These are sharpened a little differently from the other gouges discussed in the last chapter.

V-gouges are very useful, especially for carving details, although sharpening them can sometimes be a challenge.

Chisels

The carver's chisel is beveled on both sides, unlike the chisel that cabinetmakers and carpenters use, which is flat on one side and ground at a 25-degree angle on the other. Cabinetmaker's chisels are designed for paring the straight, flat edges of woodworking joints. Because of the shape of the cutting angle, you cannot carve very well with them. They tend to dig in or skip out of the wood, depending on which side you are using.

Carving chisels are beveled on both sides at a 20-degree angle. This allows you to carve at a more efficient angle and remove chips cleanly. These flat chisels, often designated as sweep no. 1, are used to set in straight lines on relief carvings or to smooth the surface of a rounded shape, such as the top edge of the wing on an American eagle carving.

Carving chisels' cutting edges can be ground perpendicular to the shaft of the blade or at an angle. The angled gouges, called skew chisels, are useful for getting into corners and other narrow spaces.

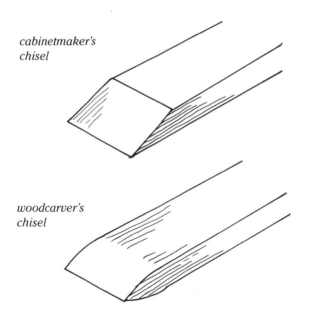

cabinetmaker's chisel

woodcarver's chisel

The difference between chisel types

From left to right: **cabinetmaker's chisel, carver's chisel, skew chisel.**

A carver's chisel is sharpened almost the same way as a knife. Put a few drops of oil on a sharpening stone for lubrication. Hold the chisel at a 20-degree angle to the stone, and slide the cutting edge up and down along the length of the stone. Work both sides of the blade evenly until a burr edge forms along the cutting edge.

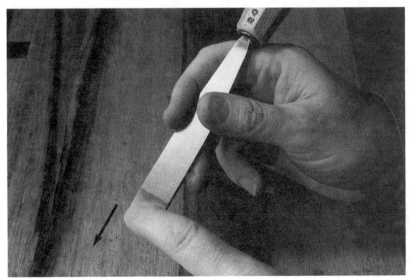

Test for the burr by very lightly dragging your finger *away* from the cutting edge. If you can feel a slight roughness, the blade is ready for the next step.

You can remove the burr edge with just a strop the same way you did with the knife, or you can use a slip stone to hone away some of the burr before the final polishing on the strop.

Hold a square ceramic slip stone at a 45-degree angle to the blade, and stroke it lightly along the cutting edge. Do this on both sides of the blade.

Then remove any remaining bits of burr edge and polish the tool with a leather strop. Draw the blade across the strop away from the cutting edge the same way you did with the knife. Work first one side of the blade and then the other until the whole burr is removed.

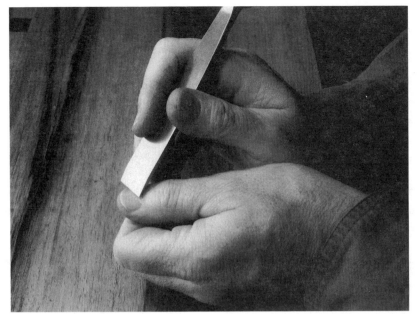

Use the fingernail to test to make sure the blade is properly sharpened before you begin carving. Just rest the cutting edge of the blade very lightly on your fingernail. If the blade skids across your nail, it needs more work. If it catches slightly or feels sticky, the blade is ready to use.

Skew chisels are sharpened the same way as straight ones, except that you hold the tool at an angle to the side of the sharpening stone so that the cutting edge is perpendicular to the length of the stone. Hold it in the same position when you strop.

V-Gouges

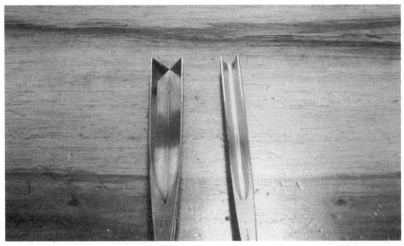

A V-gouge *(left)* is V shaped. A veiner *(right)* is U shaped.

Probably the single most useful carving tool after the knife is the V-gouge. V-gouges are invaluable for carving fine details on small figures or wildlife carvings. They are also used extensively in relief carving, both for carving details and for establishing larger shapes.

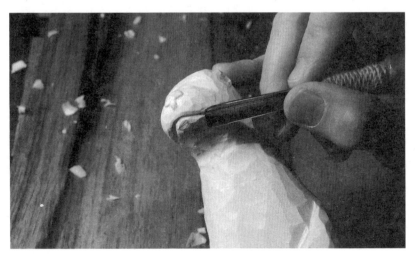

I often hold small V-gouges in a pencil grip for carving details on small carvings. Hold the blade between your thumb and index finger just like a pencil, and use these two fingers to gently push the blade through the wood. Keep the rest of your fingers braced against the wood for control, with the fingers of your other hand out of the path of the tool for safety.

Several years ago I had the opportunity to study with the woodcarvers of Brienz, Switzerland. They showed me a tip for making gouges easier to hold for carving fine details. The Swiss carvers wrap the top part of the blade with cotton or synthetic string for a better grip.

If you want to try this, just wrap a couple of layers around the shaft until it feels comfortable in your hand. I use this on any tool that I hold in a pencil grip for long periods of time. It makes carving easier and gives me more control over the tool.

Although the V-gouge is a very useful tool, it can be a challenge to sharpen—even for experienced carvers. And the V-gouge is one tool that simply won't cut unless the edge is perfect. It's best to approach the sharpening in a logical series of steps.

Begin by treating each side of the V like a flat chisel. Hold the tool at a 20-degree angle to the sharpening stone, and slide the edge back and forth along the stone until a burr edge forms. Then sharpen the other side of the V exactly the same way.

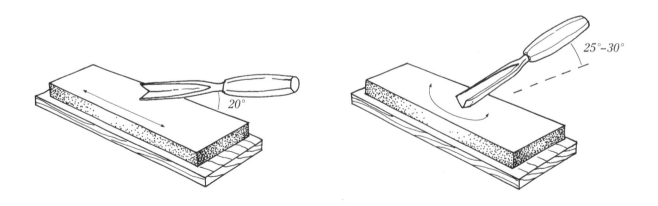

Whetting a V-gouge

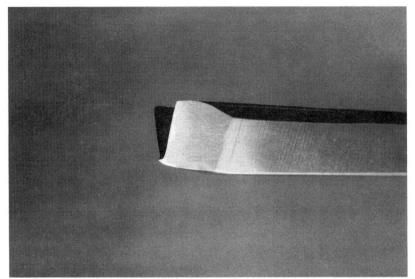

Sharpening the sides of the V-gouge produces a small hook of metal where the sides of the V meet. This hook has to be removed before you can carve, otherwise it will act as a plow and tear through the wood fibers, producing a ragged cut.

Remove the hook by treating the bottom of the V like a tiny gouge. Rock it back and forth on the stone at a 25- to 30-degree angle the same way as described for the curved gouges.

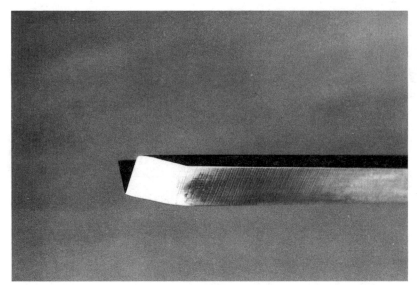

Be careful not to remove too much metal when you do this, or you can end up with a notch where the hook was. Sometimes it helps to use a triangular slip stone to sharpen away the last remnants of the hook from the inside bevel. This is how the V-gouge looks with the hook removed.

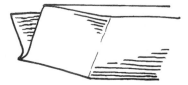

V-gouge before and after removing hook

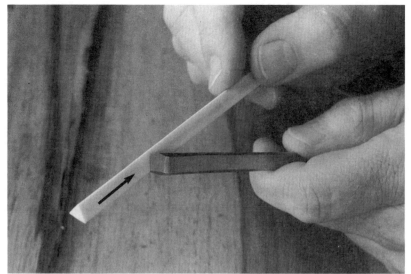

At this point, the V-gouge still has a burr edge along the sides and bottom of the inner bevel. The burr must be removed before the gouge will cut cleanly. Use an angled slip stone or a small triangular ceramic stone to hone the inside edges of the V. Hold the slip at a 45-degree angle to the blade, and then lightly slide it toward the cutting edge.

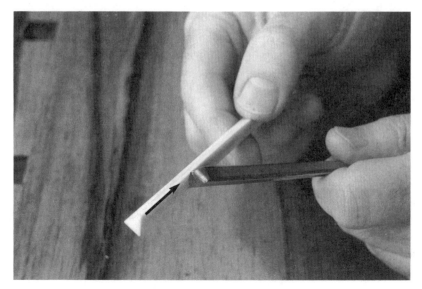

After a few passes on the inner bevel, use the flat side of the same slip stone on the outer bevel.

To remove the last traces of the burr edge and polish the blade, strop the sides of the V.

Then strop the bottom of the V like a miniature curved gouge. Always strop *away* from the cutting edge, or the tool will cut into the leather and become dulled.

Stropping the inner bevel of the V-gouge can be a little tricky. A strop with an angled side that reaches down into the V works best.

Alternatively, you can use the edge of a piece of leather to polish the inside bevel. Rub a little abrasive along the edge before you use it. This also works for stropping tiny V-gouges, such as those 3mm in width or smaller. If necessary, trim the leather with a sharp knife to get a sharply angled edge that will fit into the V.

notched edge caused by wearing away too much metal when removing the hook

cutting edge is not perpendicular to the shaft; the point will tear the wood fibers before the sides can cut them free, resulting in a jagged cut

V-gouge sharpening problems

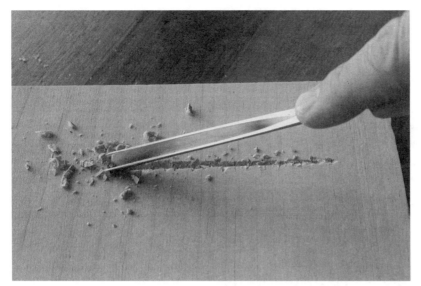

Before you begin carving, always test your V-gouge for sharpness by making a cut across the grain on a scrap piece of softwood. A dull V-gouge will tear the wood and leave a ragged cut.

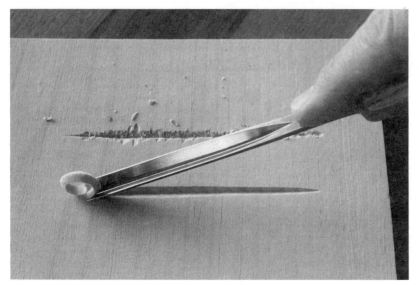

But if properly sharpened, it will leave a crisp, clean, V-shaped cut in the wood. It takes a little practice to learn how to sharpen a V-gouge correctly. But the results are well worth it.

Macaroni Tools

Macaroni tools are specialized relatives of V-gouges. The cutting edge of this tool is box shaped, and it functions like a flat gouge and a V-gouge combined.

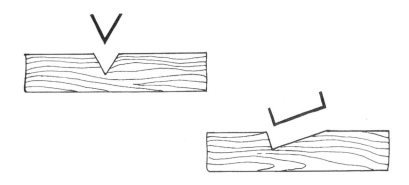

Although it looks like it is designed to cut a square channel in the wood, it is best used like a V-gouge, to incise lines in wood. The long, flat side at the bottom of the cutting edge makes creating a smooth bevel easier. This illustration shows the difference between the cuts made by a V-gouge and by a macaroni tool.

A macaroni tool is not essential, but if you have one, you will find it useful for many different styles of carving. When carving an American eagle, for example, you can use it to outline the feathers on the wing. The macaroni tool can create the shape in one step. Otherwise, you would have to first incise a line with a V-gouge, then use a flat no. 2 gouge to pare down one side of the cut to create the effect of overlapping feathers.

I also use macaroni tools to rough out small woodcarvings. They are especially helpful for blocking out the arms and legs of small figures.

Note: the carving is fastened securely to the bench, leaving both hands free to hold the gouge.

For sharpening purposes, it helps to think of the macaroni tool as two V-gouges combined, and handle it the same way you did the V-gouge. First, work the three flat sides on the sharpening stone at a 20-degree angle until a burr edge forms.

Then treat each corner like the bottom of the V-gouge, by whetting it on the sharpening stone at a 25- to 30-degree angle with a rocking motion as though it were a tiny gouge.

Remove most of the burr edge using a square slip stone. Do the inner bevel first, and then the outer bevel. Finish removing the burr and polish the tool with a leather strop. Use the flat side of the strop on the outer bevel and the angled side inside the tool.

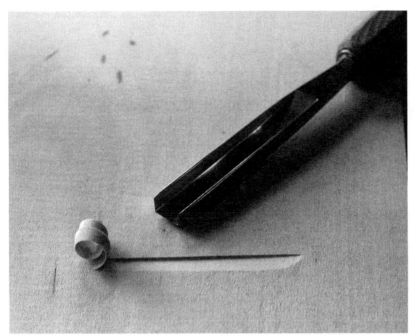

Test the macaroni tool for sharpness by making a cut across the grain on a scrap piece of softwood like pine or basswood. If it cuts cleanly, you are ready for carving. If you decide to add a macaroni tool to your collection, you will be surprised how often it comes in handy. It is well worth the little extra time it takes to sharpen.

Veiners

The veiner is a gouge that cuts a U-shaped groove in wood. It gets its name from medieval times, when carved foliage was used for decorating churches and other important buildings. Popular Gothic motifs were acanthus and grape leaves, and the U shape was perfect for carving the veins in them, hence the name veiner.

Today we carve less foliage, but the veiner is still a very useful tool. It is frequently used in relief carving to make deep, narrow cuts that have a more rounded profile than those made with a V-gouge. This gives a softer appearance to incised lines when viewed from a distance.

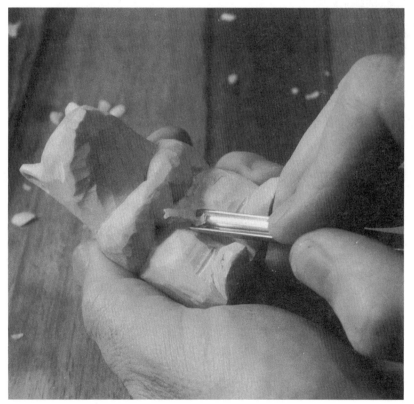

The veiner is also good for detailing small carvings. I use veiners on Santa Claus carvings to make the fur ruffs on the hat and cloak look soft and fluffy. I also find it handy when carving animals. It's great for removing wood from narrow spaces, such as between the hind paws of this chipmunk.

Veiners combine the straight sides of a V-gouge with the rounded bottom of a curved gouge, and the technique for sharpening is also a hybrid between the two.

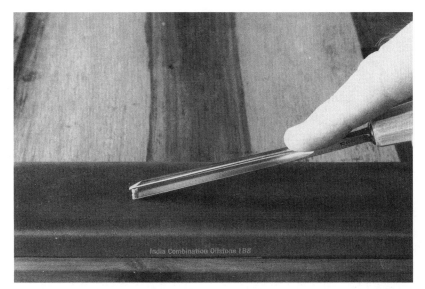

Sharpen the flat sides at a 20-degree angle the same way you would a flat carver's chisel. Slide them up and down the sharpening stone until a burr edge forms.

Then sharpen the curved portion by rocking it on the stone like a gouge at a 25- to 30-degree angle.

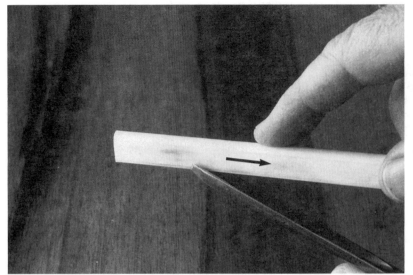

Next, use slip stones to hone the edge and remove most of the burr. It may be difficult to find a slip that fits the inner curve of the veiner exactly. If necessary, use a slip with a narrow, rounded shape and rotate it along the length of the cutting edge. Hold the slip at a 45-degree angle to the blade, and slide it toward the cutting edge.

Use the flat side of the slip stone to hone the outer bevel.

Polish the outside bevel of the veiner on the flat side of the strop, rotating the tool as you draw it over the leather to bring the entire cutting edge into contact.

Use the angled edge of the strop to polish the inner bevel. The strop may not fit inside very small veiners, such as those 3mm in width or smaller.

For these tools, use a piece of stiff leather with a little abrasive grit rubbed on it as a strop. You can sand the edge of the leather to round it for a better fit.

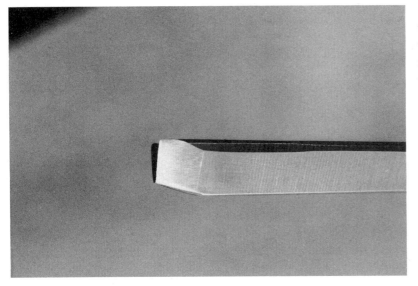

Test the veiner for sharpness the same way as described for the other tools, using the thumbnail test or making a cut across the grain on a piece of softwood.

Winged V-Gouges

Winged V-gouges are truly exotic among carving tools. Instead of being straight, the two sides of the V flare outward like curved wings.

In the days when rooms had hand-carved wooden decoration, these tools were used to carve architectural details such as grapes and fluted moldings. Winged Vs were also used to create the basic shapes for beaded and rope-shaped molding patterns.

Because of the odd shape, you cannot sharpen the winged V on a flat sharpening stone. Instead, use the curved edge of a fine India slip stone for whetting. Oil the edge of the slip, and whet each outer bevel of the winged V at a 25-degree angle until a burr forms.

Hone the burr away with ceramic slip stones. A round shape works best on the outer bevel. Work the slip against the cutting edge the same way as described for honing the bevel on the other gouges.

Use a narrow triangular slip stone to hone the inner bevel.

Test the edge for sharpness on your thumbnail or a piece of scrap softwood. Then make some practice cuts with the tool to get a feeling for how it works. A series of cuts with a sharp winged V-gouge can create attractive fluted shapes for decorative carving.

The tools discussed in this chapter are a little more difficult to sharpen than the knife and the other gouges. But once you have mastered creating a perfect edge on the V-gouge, macaroni tool, and veiner, you can consider yourself an expert at sharpening carving tools.

The art of sharpening is not difficult to learn; it just takes a little patience and perseverance. And even as an expert you will occasionally discover a tool or situation that will call for these necessary qualities. Woodcarving has a way of keeping a person humble.

Care of Tools

Good woodcarving tools are not cheap and never have been, although you can buy dozens of carving gouges for less than the cost of a single power woodworking machine. Properly cared for, woodcarving tools will give you years of enjoyment and become heirlooms to be passed down from generation to generation.

I like to keep all my tools razor sharp and ready to carve, and I always check new tools before I use them for the first time to make sure they are sharp. Some tools come sharpened, but most need at least a little work to get a perfect cutting edge. Nothing is more frustrating than being in the middle of a big carving project, reaching for a tool, and finding out you have to stop and sharpen it. It's much easier and more fun to make sure all your tools are ready first so that you can concentrate on carving.

Once all your tools are sharp, protect your investment of time and money in them. Tools tossed carelessly in the drawer of a workbench will quickly become dull and nicked. This can also happen on your bench while you are carving. The cutting edge of a knife or gouge is hard but brittle, and if it bumps against a hard object such as the shaft of another tool, it can be damaged. A nicked edge will leave a white scratch in the

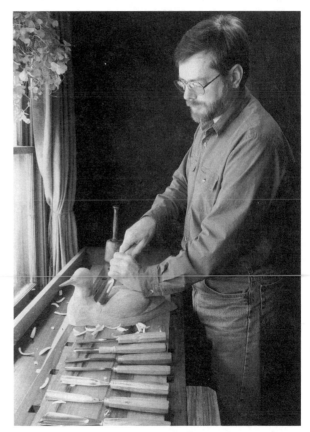

Properly cared for, woodcarving tools will last hundreds of years. Keep them organized neatly on your bench while carving to protect the cutting edges.

73

wood with each cut you make. The only way to repair the edge is to resharpen it.

To prevent this, I line up the tools I need for a project in a neat row on the bench. Usually I also lay the tools out in order of sweep number—so that when I want a particular tool I can just put out my hand and pick it up. I don't have to stop carving to hunt for it. It requires a little discipline to keep putting tools back where they belong while you are working, but it really saves a lot of time. This is a good system for protecting tools while you are carving, because all of the blades are aligned and pointed the same way, minimizing the chances of a nicked cutting edge.

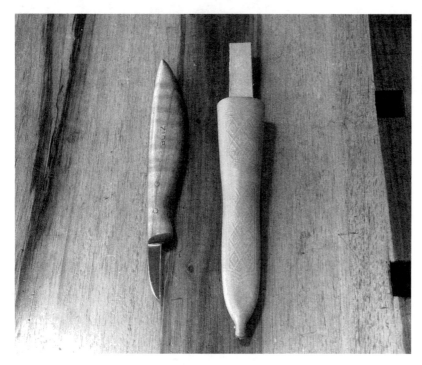

When you are not carving, there are several good ways to protect your tools. Keep your knife in a leather sheath or store it inside a cloth tool roll.

Tool rolls are usually made of heavy canvas or denim folded and sewn to form pockets. For knives and small gouges, I use a homemade tool roll with a flap that folds over the blades. Then the whole thing is rolled up into a neat bundle and tied to secure it.

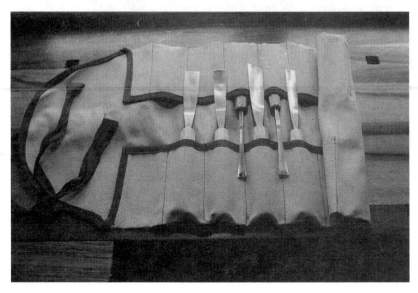

My larger gouges are protected in commercial cloth tool rolls with double pockets. This type also rolls up and is secured by ties for storage.

Another way to protect your tools is to store them in a wooden rack. This arrangement makes your gouges more accessible when you are carving. I arrange mine by size and sweep number so that it is easy to locate a particular tool when I need it. I made these tool racks with commercially available strips of molding that I found in a local lumber store. They keep all of my small and medium-size gouges safely out of the way.

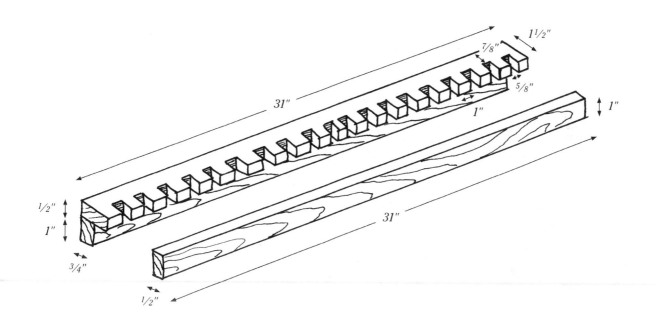

1½"

7/8"

31"

1"

5/8"

1"

½"

1"

31"

3/4"

½"

Traditional tool rack

I keep the larger gouges stored in a Swiss-style tool rack, where they wedge nicely behind wood crossbars. You can easily make a tool holder like this from scrap pieces of wood along with a piece of plywood for the back section.

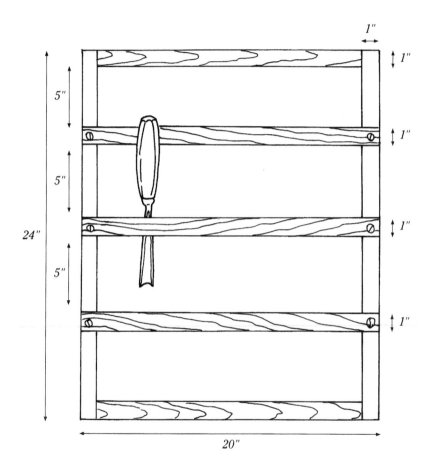

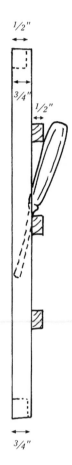

Swiss-style tool rack

If carefully stored, woodcarving tools require little maintenance. Every few months the blades and handles should be wiped down with a thin coating of 3-in-One household oil to protect them from moisture. Rust is a common problem that is encouraged by the salt and acid from fingerprints. If a rust spot appears on a tool, just rub it smooth with #000 steel wool and wipe it down with a thin layer of light household oil.

Sometimes it also helps to smooth down the wooden handles of new tools with 280 grit sandpaper or #000 steel wool. This removes any rough spots in the finish caused by dust or wood fibers embedded in the varnish. Afterward, wipe the handle with a coat of boiled linseed oil, allow it to soak into the wood for a few hours, and then wipe the excess completely off. This creates a smooth, easy-to-grip finish that ages to a mellow patina over the years.

Restoring Antique Woodcarving Tools

You may have the good fortune to acquire antique gouges to use. Often these work quite well, depending on their condition. Personally I have always liked working with old tools. It gives me a sense of being in touch with the past, of being part of the ancient tradition of woodcarving.

Some carvers believe that the steel was of better quality in the older tools. Generally, however, I've found that modern steel has a higher, more consistent quality, although much depends on the manufacturer, regardless of the age of the tool.

There is one trait of some older woodcarving gouges that you should be aware of, however. Blacksmiths and tool manufacturers in the eighteenth and nineteenth centuries had difficulty achieving a balance between the hardness and resiliency of their tool steel. They wanted a hardened cutting edge for lasting sharpness, but the shaft had to be softer and more flexible or it would break under the strain. They solved this problem by tempering, or heat treating, the blade so that the steel was hard and brittle at the cutting edge but progressively softer along the shaft.

Therefore, any antique carving gouge where the blade has been worn down is probably into the softer steel and won't hold a sharp edge. This is usually the case if the blade is shorter than 3 to 3½ inches in length. Old woodcarvers were expected to know how to retemper their own tools when they wore down, but few people have that skill anymore. With modern tools this is not a problem, because the improved steel alloys can be tempered to a consistent hardness along the full length of the blade.

So look for antique carving tools with a full blade, 4½ to 6 inches long, depending on the maker. Such tools are often fine pieces of steel that can perform as well as any modern tool.

To restore old tools, first clean off any rust with #000 steel wool and light oil. Clean the handles with some mineral spirits and extrafine #0000 steel wool to remove any accumulated grime. Then wipe the tool down with a thin layer of light oil, such as 3-in-One, and you are ready to sharpen it. Be sure to dispose of any oily rags in sealed metal containers to prevent the risk of fire from spontaneous combustion.

Repairing Chipped Edges

Sometimes an old tool, or even a new one, will have a badly nicked edge, usually from being dropped on a hard surface. This can actually break off a piece of the cutting edge. The only cure is to grind the edge flat and then resharpen it. To do so, you can use the coarse black side of an India combination stone with oil as a lubricant. Simply hold the tool perpendicular to the stone, and rub it back and forth until the cutting edge is straight and even. Then sharpen the edge as you normally would.

If you have one, a wet grinding wheel will save you a lot of time. These abrasive wheels are turned by geared-down electric motors, or by hand, so that they rotate at a speed no greater than 100 revolutions per minute (RPM). They are usually a medium-fine grit and range in size from 6 to 10 inches in diameter. To keep them wet, they are partially submerged in a trough of water. This ensures that the grinding surface is always lubricated with a thin film of water. The slow speed and the water are important because they cool the edge of the gouge during the grinding process.

Hold the tool against the grinding stone with a steady, medium-firm pressure. You don't need to press too hard; let the stone do the cutting. When the cutting edge of the tool has been ground to a straight surface, sharpen it as you normally would.

Do not use any type of dry electric grinding wheel for your carving tools. These grinders, which are found in many garages and workshops, turn at speeds in excess of 1000 RPM, and the friction quickly overheats the metal and ruins the temper. This permanently softens the metal so that the tool will not stay sharp and will dull quickly in use. Some carvers suggest using these high-speed grinders and repeatedly dipping the tool blade in water to keep it cool. Even with this method, I have still found that it is very easy to overheat the steel and ruin the edge of the tool. I don't recommend it.

So remember: Take good care of your tools and they will give you a lifetime of service and enjoyment.

Resources

The Tools You Need and How to Sharpen Them
with Rick Bütz
    WMHT
    Book and Video Sales
    P.O. Box 17
    Schenectady, NY 12301
    (800) 950-9648
    Sixty-minute instructional video

Woodcraft
    210 Wood County Industrial Park
    P.O. Box 1686
    Parkersburg, WV 26102-1682
    (800) 225-1153
    knives, gouges, sharpening stones, strops

Woodcarvers Supply, Inc.
    P.O. Box 7500
    Englewood, FL 34295-7500
    (800) 284-6229
    knives, gouges, sharpening supplies

Albert Constantine & Sons
    2050 Eastchester Rd.
    Bronx, NY 10461
    (718) 792-1600
    woodcarving tools and sharpening supplies

National Wood Carvers Association
    7424 Miami Ave.
    Cincinnati, OH 45243
    dues include a subscription to Chip Chats, *a bi-monthly magazine filled with projects, patterns, and regional news about woodcarving*

ABOUT THE AUTHORS

Rick Bütz, who brings some thirty years' carving experience to Stackpole's Woodcarving Step by Step series, recently served as host of the popular PBS series "Woodcarving with Rick Bütz." **Ellen Bütz** is a woodcarver, writer, and photographer; she and Rick have written numerous articles on carving for *Fine Woodworking, Woodworker's Journal, Wood Magazine,* and others. They are also the authors of *How to Carve Wood* and *Woodcarving with Rick Bütz.* They live in a log cabin in the Adirondack Mountains of New York State.